By Terry Stokes

Natural Disasters   1971
Crimes of Passion   1973

Crimes of Passion

TERRY STOKES

CRIMES OF PASSION

Alfred A. Knopf   New York   1973

![borzoi logo]

This is a Borzoi Book published by Alfred A. Knopf, Inc.
Published in the United States
by Alfred A. Knopf, Inc., New York,
and simultaneously in Canada
by Random House of Canada Limited, Toronto.
Distributed by Random House, Inc., New York.

Library of Congress Cataloging in Publication Data
Stokes, Terry.   Crimes of passion.
Poems.
I. Title.
PS3569.T622C7   811'.5'4   72-8978
ISBN 0-394-48251-4
ISBN 0-394-70797-4 (pbk.)
Manufactured in the United States of America
First Edition

The author wishes to thank the following magazines
in which some of the poems in this collection first appeared:
*Antaeus, The Carleton Miscellany, Chelsea,
Diana's Bi-Monthly, Esquire, Ironwood, La Huerta,
The Nation, New American Review, The New Yorker,
New York Quarterly, North American Review,
Shuttle, Skywriting, Sumac, The Young American Poets*
and the following presses which have published
some of the poems as broadsides or booklets:
Baby John Press, Burning Deck Press,
Cat's Pajamas Press, and Western Review Press.

for Linda

Contents

Crimes of Passion

All Morning

All morning a wren has been building
a nest in my ear. I will shelter anyone

who needs it, it's always been
my problem, & who can resist small

birds? They cannot hurt you,
even their tail feathers

twitching like soft razor blades,
my friend, oh, my friend.

Snake Fences

The fields take on ten inches of snow
as if they were dreaming, dreaming

a white sauce & were the bellies of
a thousand good fish, but the table

is crowded & we are sobbing away our
lives, the impossibility, wings

splinter in green light, teeth of
the dead woman having ingested

the whole winter one night, this is
a restful dinner, or so she thought,

a red star snaps in the corner of her eye,
hot fur stumbles up the long hall
of her spine.

Encounter
Out In The Open

In the open gold field, that monotonous
spring afternoon, we talked of
binoculars, & swamps. Oh, & the way
in which desperation hits
in your hands & winds up back
in the spine, roots
in your teeth yanked
by a very strong & sadistic
torturer. I tried to explain this,
the vines do not tangle
in your flesh
with such a flourish &
the combat I encounter is
never clear. You could not buy
my story of ambush outright,
there was some checking to be done, as if
tanks could actually fly off the trails,
& anger is furnished with the clothing
at the Army-Navy store.

The grenades in my heart, you called,
pineapples, you dismantled them, saying,
your fingers were not always this steady,
we ate everything on the moist earth,
including the intelligence report.
The disarmament talks
continue to run smoothly, a fine
warm line rises between us, the red
sun bleeds in the dark trees.

Rain

All day I spent
with water. I rained
nasturtiums, I rained
hearts of mushrooms, my
eyes were cocktail waitresses
weeping into avocado dip—there
are days frequently moaning

the slow rivers are cheap white bread
the slow rivers are boiled tomatoes
the slow rivers are broad veins
in my teeth, my teeth without tears
the slow rivers fondle themselves
like candle drippings

We move into each other, gauze
without wounds, soaking up
the blood & water of our lives.

Straightening Up

Your whole heart can fail. You
can be a hundred years old in May &
still walk to work or cut down trees.
You can fly through the swollen mirror,
eat sour blue hornets, spit up
the glowing foetus. You can
blackmail lawyers attempting
to straighten up your life. You
can rewrite your arms & legs on sidewalks
as the milk curdles in the sun. You
can fall in love with the priest
of the forest & ask him to
marry you every leap year, the wood
whining & tired. You can fashion
funnels out of your favorite bodies, toss
the trash down, let them learn
a little something from the snarled
cans, the over-whelming desire
to eat & drink &
complicate several
layers of earth.

Getting Lost On Friday

Surely, a classy bar
several hot truck drivers
collect their thoughts.
Pinballs rattle like dislocated testicles,
& record on the flashing board,
& free game, bam, free game, bam, free game, bam,
& a beer glass flares like the sun.
We inhale their smoky voices, sore,
their teeth bite clear through our tonsils,
they are coming for our quiet children.

They Are Animals

Six ducklings on the four-lane road
& the mother
& the mother
watches the small balls
of blood & feathers
bounce
they are bouncing off the trees

they are bouncing off my eyes
I take them home
I make a home for them
I mother/father six ducks

they are animals & do not think
"this is one hell of a place,"
as the hardy steel
vehicles
collide with their fragile eyes.

Thanksgiving: 1970

"The weed of crime bears bitter fruit"—Lamont Cranston

1 I pick up the *Tribune,* see that everything
in the world has gone wrong. One girl

behind the drug counter, her after-school
job, St. Paul, "In Jesus's name,

don't take this money. I have the truth
of God. I'm walking with God. He has something

that could help you." The stick-up man
wandered out into the boring night after saying,

"Thank you." She also said, "I don't know
if God helped the robber, but he sure helped me."

The Pilgrims were really happy that the Injuns
showed them how to fix corn, without corn

it just wouldn't have been a real Thanksgiving.
But corn cooking, & Divine favor, well,

there isn't any comparison, & with Christ
committing big crimes is impossible. Is love

in any form wrong? Is an empty stomach
a dream? He who fills his body with junk

comes close to nibbling on the legs of the Lord.
The Pilgrims at eight, "It's time to go back

to the ghetto, my friends, here, read The Book,
you're bound to get something out of it,

oh, & thanks for the corn, & the tobacco,
but, you know, we don't smoke."

2 Secretary of Defense Melvin R. Laird testified
today that he recommended the U.S. raid on a

North Vietnamese prisoner-of-war camp because,
"Our men were dying in captivity."

The Indians occupying Alcatraz began their second
year on the island in San Francisco yesterday,

still determined to get the United States to
deed it to them for an Indian culture center.

If the Indians "start attacking boats with bows
and arrows again or precipitate some other trouble,"

they may be removed by force. Life for the occupying
Indians is austere. "It's not too hard. If you

have lived on a reservation you have experienced
these same hardships." The children spend their

time playing Indian games or taking classes
in bead-making and Indian lore.

Under an 1869 treaty with the Sioux the Indians
went on reservations but were entitled to

any land the government later abandoned. The
government says Alcatraz has not been abandoned but

"is merely temporarily out of use." For a time
they had only candles for light.

Mr. Laird said, "it is my firm belief that the lives
of our American prisoners are in danger every day."

3 In Barcelona, stuffed cabbage at midnight.
   All day I have been under the impression

   my sister has given birth to a son in New York.
   I hold the blue telegram in my hand,

   it is warm, the black print says, yes. A second
   helping of stuffed cabbage. I lose sleep in an

   uncomfortable foreign bed. Barcelona sighs.
   Gaudi's building oozes toward me like a hot

   gray serpent, out for lunch. Buy a book of
   translations, have coffee and brandy, know

   everything I taste is seedless. Ride a train
   through endless fields, they glow, green,

   my heart sags, blood dries in my veins,
   blood drags on in my prayers.

The Night
Of The Big Fight

The night of the big fight
we listened to poetry, had

a late dinner at Cleopatra's.
The owner's ears were stuffed

grape leaves, I would have offered
you a bite, but I didn't know him very well

then, & I was more concerned with your eyes,
delicious vegetables, sprouting,

right before me, a whole garden, you
know, I was like a rabbit, refilling

my plate over & over, never
able to diminish my appetite, until

later, holding you against death
in the off-white room, thinking

of Stonehenge, the rocks splitting
our lives, the winter solstice

coming soon, perhaps we will
dine on the shadows, ancient Druids

dressed for that serious event.

The Night Ed Sullivan Slapped
One Of The Kessler Twins
Right On The Ass
In The Middle Of His Show
& Their Song & Dance

1 He apologized right away. & she said
   it was o.k., that he hadn't hurt anything.
   Succulent in tight gold lamé,
   & enough there
   moving
   to slap all the way
   to some downtown bed. & maybe
   old Ed was thinking, too.

2 He apologized right away. & she said
   it was o.k., that a little pain in the ass
   was nothing. Nothing.

3 He apologized right away. & she said
   it was o.k., it wasn't a slap
   in the face, & skies are orange
   over the city, & warm, god, warm.

4 He apologized right away. & she said
   it was o.k., my torrid flesh
   carries your hand print upon it
   & the night is careless
   & knows no magic
   though a hundred-million eyes
   weep through my pants.

5 He apologized right away. & she said
   it was o.k., & her sister said,
   me, high-kicker, & pretty, too,
   give me a hand.

6 He apologized right away. & she said
   it was o.k.

I Won't Explain

The car is not big enough to be a home,
so, I took off the wheels, nosed & decked
it, painted it panther black, I won't
explain. I filled it full of water,
& I gave the water plenty of large pink salmon,
I put the windshield wipers on, & planted
the whole thing in the snow. At night,
the interior lights hot, the children
circle, saying small prayers, as if
they were speaking to their lovely, but
lost, mother.

The Net

Black dress, hood, black shoes,
she sits on the chair on the shore
in the sun. She weaves fishing nets,
she has five miles now, but her old fingers
keep twisting, a year from now

some new man arrives, "Is that
for me?" She clucks, hides her
eyes, her face in black, & offers
everything, the loose cords
drifting on the water.

The Pet Parade

Marching. We played music.
Down the mainstreet.

I was not very good, I never
practiced, but I liked to march

& ice cream. Next to me,
more clarinets. A girl,

"Hey Tits," somebody in the crowd
knew her name.

We puffed on to the park.

Mentioning James Dean

1 "Who?"

2 Lilacs drifted into my nostrils
like small dirigibles. I brushed
my twelve-year-old haircut carefully.
The impossibility of talking to anyone,
so you mumble, sometimes you whine, but
some things you will outgrow. All of us
have tripped into dark rooms, banging
into still objects, sweating, &
there she was—Mother,
rabbit sounds squirt, come
from inside of your eyes, squinting,
the pain of new light
shredded in thin air.

3 They saw your body in dreams. They saw
it intact, your face blown off or
a clown's, & holding services
they knew you were among them, scrambling
for some sweet love, flesh, or
just a friend's arm, & the swollen
park on Sundays.

4 You took a wrong turn, but
we followed, our eyes nailed
to the bone screen. Take us
back, or let us
feel the seance table
fall apart in our dead fingers.

The Man

What I can get for you
is big things, really big things,
not only are they big, they are warm,
you have probably heard about things
like this, eh? You have heard maybe
in the yellow pages, or as you pissed
in your pants, lost, but happy, walking
around Grand Central Station, looking
up at the moving ads & the revolving cars,
you have heard about such things, you
put your hand on them, & they stick, the
flesh inside your spine is hot hamburg,
Ah, you like that feeling, & you touch
some more, & you get crazy, touching, &
these things take a liking to you, too,
you think maybe you can take them home,
well, look, it goes this way, I give you,
I mean, I give you these things, yes, these
things that make your tendons stretch
with anguish, exquisite, eh? Yes, I give
you, & you pay a little every month,
& that will be good, you will like the
deal, of course, you are a hard worker,
you believe your home should be outfitted
like that, right? Sure, we shake on it, now,
like gentlemen.

Getting The Company
To Back Our Relationship

What can be written off?
Everything? Nothing? What's included,

part-time mismanagement, entertainment,
all the things easily jotted

in small figures on a secret pad,
A Dreamburger, & fries, in a suffocating

lounge, complete with round orange
globes, burning on the ceiling,

& what I was saying about your make-up
that morning, the absence of your make-up,

a clumsy compliment, I am very facile
with that area. Write it off.

Through the accounting department
I have requested your love, I have

asked for monthly shipments, in plain
brown wrappers, not wanting to disturb

anyone else along the line. They have
asked for references, & I'm stuck

wandering through the statues of
your lovers, slapping them on the back,

buying beers, trying to cheer
them up, without offending, tho

bizarre smiles cling to my face, &
electric fish in my eyes

spill my heart, jolting them.
It is good for a woman to be wanted

this way; pink forms dribble from my pockets,
I come toward you, arms open

for business, lady.

Immigrant Theater

I think nothing
of the braids trapped in her hair,
I think so little in the wind.

When I came to the big shore
I thought of many things,
I thought of men & women
with hankies in their pockets, &
suppositories, but that was Europe,
& I never felt at home there.

Look, I have tasted the fat melon
of warm felt, I know what it is to
be nineteen & excited over something,
did you ever see the butterfly
collection in my pocket? Ah well,
& when you let them live good, they
pee on your hands, it's always that
way. The kids, the kids are rattling
in their walls, they are beating
each other with love, & fragile whips, one
swore the other day
soon the building would fall
on us, we deserved it, our hostess
cupcakes, our vaginal sprays, & what
we do to ourselves behind newspapers
with our hands of speed, I am not
so certain anymore. To be happy,
what brains it takes, to be rich or
borrow flesh, that is not all wrong or
good. On the wall where I lived, "We
meet old age without dismay, and death
is sweet at last." On the wall where I lived,
ice & fat red flies. On the wall where
I lived, whole continents of happy women
dressed to kill, some naked, some not.
On the wall where I lived, toothpicks, &

razor blades, steaming in the sun. On the
wall where I lived, my mother dead in
the stomach with me. On the wall where
I lived, hot bastard snakes, eyes of
runny glue. On the wall where I
lived, stone fingers in her hair,
stone fingers in her flesh.

Crimes Of Passion:
The Phone Caller

No, no, don't, please,
oh my warm chicken, do
not be upset, & do not
hang up, what I wish to
say can only be spoken
in low tones, no, tonight
I won't groan, I groan
only when I am unhappy, do
you understand? If I throw
a kiss into your ears, who
knows? & who cares? That is
the problem, what you learn
of loneliness, I teach, & I
teach it slowly, so you will
understand fully. I am chewing
on a carrot, & I am thinking of
nothing but you, I am thinking
of you quietly, putting out
tomorrow's clothes, tomorrow
you will wear the red sweater
which causes your breasts to be
like carrots. & you will come
down the stairs at 7:46, & you
will squint & put on your purple
oval sunglasses, & trying to
appear quite casual, you will
look up the street, you will
look down the street, you will
pause one second, & sigh, &
when that look of relief covers
your face, I will step out of
the morning, drag you into the warm
alley, & there with what's left
of this carrot, I will hurt you
very badly, but of course I will
kiss you ever so gently first,
with all my heart.

Crimes Of Passion:
The Slasher

What I like most is when
the hemline rises
& they place the high heel,
usually the right,
onto the first step of the bus,
then, they grasp the small
rod, & pull themselves up. The nylons
flare like hot butter, & as that
thigh bulges slightly, & then
taut, I gently nudge her
& with the razor blade, one side
taped, as if a finger
were lovingly running from the back
of the knee toward the buttocks.
She will sometimes turn & smile,
feeling some part of herself freed,
only hours later does she learn
how deep my passion runs, the thick
blood of birth drips silently
to some cold floor,
& in that pool, my face returns
the wonderful smile, & then, I think,
she probably screams. She will dream of me,
& that is all
anyone can ever ask.

Hunting Season

1 It is marble hunting. A wing
of a small bird, gone berserk
tearing open a window.
Against the white marble,
a design so intricate
to call it other
than death
is false. There are bottoms
to everything,
including the star
which pinches
the corner of the grave.

2 Monumental cottonballs
come
to close up my throat for the winter.

3 You nod your head,
& close your eyes,
& a long walk in the wind.
You haven't begun the dream, yet.
A pragmatic indian
is a dead indian
in any man's culture. This I know.
The stories float from mouth
to ear to etchings in the sky
for all to read. Fires
burn earth words
like so much thin bark
in the warm rain.

4 Gutter water rattles
  & will never make the sea.
  A woman, as always, wanders
  a path to the river,
  & hunched in her own shadows
  she scrubs the soil from the clothing.
  It will dry rapidly in the sun,
  on the rocks,
  as she watches
  the distance, & winces,
  a squirrel is storing food
  a thousand years away.

5 I have gone all through this house
  borrowing language from devils.
  You, who harness trees & expect movement,
  find a moon who will love you,
  take her home, wrap her in clear paper,
  set her in a window
  so someone will know how you feel.
  I am lost in these few rooms,
  the paint swells with poison,
  I bind twelve scarlet feathers,
  & take on the walls
  frothing at the mouth.

A Man Called Horse,
&/or several other things

1 We see the gods mumbling through
their business, tripping

but they are the ones who rip
the spears from our hands,

make us smile on dusty mornings
when the horses are quiet,

the voices of wolves come
from wolves, this is a good day,

one old woman is always foraging,
another needs a husband, & Christ

somebody dies if it gets cold out,
& everything, the ritual, my blood

will soak into the earth, my
blood will be tasted by the gods,

there is no need to speak, speaking
happens often enough.

2 If you don't find your way clear
on a day like this, it will never

happen. I have seen many men
lolled by the Big Hands, perhaps

even their thighs stroked
& they murmur, & after a while

they are scalping other men, twisting
knives into flesh like their lives

depended on it. Does this sound
familiar? It is a dream we pass

on to the braves as it comes their time
& butterflies sag into the mud.

3 The day is red. It is red
  this day. Red red.

  The sun is red. The rocks,
  red. Red,

  the glimmer, shield of sky.

4 I collect my information from the wind,
  I collect my information from the heart.

  What is murky was murky.
  What is a dream but a reminder

  of a thousand we've led, beyond
  our bodies. Painted differently

  & muscles shift, we are soft
  & the taste of flower petals

  glows through our teeth, a delight
  to have been this close to someone

  not understanding a word she utters,
  not even understanding the subtlety

  of a smile, the hips
  are a line, the horizon, & small purple clouds

  puff like smoke, off there
  in the distance, perhaps a thousand years ago.

  The rocks suffer, I hear them
  mutter every night. All night.

The History Of Tangled Wires

Some nights I wish there were
late phone calls to be made,

red aluminum streamers spitting out,
covering the situation, bushes

of static, flower, the team of operators
falling in love with me, making

the most expensive person-to-person call ever,
in the history of their tangled wires,

& they know, christ, they know
I'm plugging myself into your wasteland

voice, plugging myself into the shreds
of your lost loves, I offer my dialing

finger as collateral, they say it is
sufficient, tho I will never be allowed

a call such as this ever again,
I mumble, getting wound up, it wasn't my idea,

Ah, hah, they say, returning a thousand years
of change, this line is busy, tied up

forever, & stop bothering people who want to sleep,
lover, sleep.

Finally Paying Certain Bills

Stuck with magnets to a board in the kitchen: Bills.
Coal, telephone, electric, food charges
at the general store, all past due.
A game my stepfather used to play,
wanting us all crazy, at loose ends.

Hand puppets mother shaped for months.
Wolves. & I couldn't be happy.
& it was Christmas, & we were frightened
enough of our lives
to be Christians. We knew about blood.
I asked only
perfection; claiming simplicity of lines
in all the fabrics which surrounded me.
How long will a person with a limited imagination
find wolves attractive?

Chips in glasses bothered me.
& how was it possible my mother could love
a man whose brain was so many shattered windows
encased in a garbage can. I would chuck pebbles
to rattle him a little; run my fingernails
down a pane, so the whole world
screeched with so many garbage cans even
the most efficient garbage man
couldn't keep up the good work.

She would let him throw her shaky body
against the dark walls. Her cracked skull
saving my already cracked teeth.
Phone calls: mother in a hospital wrapped in white gauze;
stepfather locked in white in jails, hospitals,
where I knew they would break him.
It always came back to the fact
that I wouldn't let chipped things rest;
wanting, at least, to direct the way the pieces fell.

I can't stand the crookedness of the pictures I draw.
I stain my clothing like all old men do
having caught up with their reflections.

The Gout King

*"When that pain splits my toe,
I will sigh happily, heaven at hand"—The Gout King*

He gets up, big round morning,
the pulse of whiskey

still flashing a wounded wild turkey
behind my eyes, & says,

"How about some refried beans & hot peppers?"
I mumble something into my hands,

not wanting to offend anyone,
the spaghetti of the night before

flying like red caterpillars
committing suicide,

throwing themselves against my throat,
"or maybe some tamales?" & I rise,

a Christ fumbling with a rocky morning,
I kiss the whore of a toilet with deep gratitude,

just having been there
was quite enough.

This book

is sent to you with our compliments.

We would appreciate receiving

two copies of any mention of it

which you may publish.

But no review should appear

before publication date .

```
TITLE:      CRIMES OF PASSION
AUTHOR:     Terry Stokes
PRICE:      $4.95 (also available in
            Knopf paper, $1.95)
PUB DATE:   February 19th
```

Alfred A. Knopf, Inc.

201 East Fiftieth Street, New York City 10022

This Is No Way

arms are not tunnels
for wires, & yet
when you roll over
I feel the heart in my head
buzz a thousand miles away.
No one has ever
wanted
without words, but
you quote me
before I open my mouth. These
words are small fish
on thighs, they swim, red,
to kiss the tangled darkness
of your body. I step into
the shadows where our children grow,
they peer through your eyes,
waking me with silent
fingers, & full voices.

The Ballad Of Loose Teeth

The Ballad Of Loose Teeth was
playing, a song, a movie, about

a character's life. A slippery
adolescent, the time he got

walloped by the retarded, & long
kid in the green halls of the grammar

school, it had been such a
complicated life until the slow motion

fist was caught in the exciting close-up.
Scenes shift quickly, & with more integrity,

the kind of integrity we insist upon
when we're lost in a movie, or holding on

to any fat edge of illusion
which sometimes couples with a

back-breaking single in the ninth, you
thought you'd slip one by the scrawny

shortstop who hadn't had a hit in 56
trips to the plate, oh, the aspirin

tablets you serve balloon, & people
fall flat & wonder why the teeth

weren't put in better in the first
place, & the soggy knife pushes

beyond bone, beyond the first
twinge of certain pain.

Beyond The Terrible Waters

The oil slides back on the water.
The pictures, blue, black, stop.
The stream is quiet, dark green, &
when I lift myself, I am drawing
an Indian scream from the woods.

I said, I would go home, find
a solid trunk to gather into my arms.
I said, I would stay away from water, &
the water which is ice. I said to you,
walking underwater toward the deeper underwater,
& the fish with eyes of kumquats, & skin
of breadfruit, do not speak to me
now, I am outside, I am
taking on the great toad mother, &
the things which split trees.

There are always water ceremonies.
& there are trees with rotted roots
glowing, & I said, I will never
speak to you in dream voice, or let
owls interrupt love-making. But in the rain,
inside the rain, we crawl into the plants,
& follow the stretch marks as they cut into
the mother.

Oh, I have no heart but the heart
of the dead bird. Last night, I took
it in. I did not know its name, or what
it did, & I was hungry, perhaps never this hungry.
The feathers, red, still stick in my teeth.
I feel when I swallow, this bird continues.
My throat is wing-scratched & dirty
with the dream.

When the storm comes
they still sing in the forest,
we have built one beyond the terrible waters.

The Saint

A thousand ruthless oranges
glow in the trees.
Children even eat the skin.
& their bellies light up
as they play World War III
with their very best friends.

I grow oranges anywhere I can.
Today, they sprout
through
houses, fun-rooms,
spreading the taste of flesh.

As I sow my seeds, vitamins,
I hear a thousand children
screaming for the taut orange skins.

Through The Window

Outside, & three stories down,
shadows chuck themselves, snow at one another.

& the streetlights waver, grieve
into the night.

A season of lost voices
is upon us.

Things To Do
In The Country

Watch the light from the house
behind this house
crawl into the stream.

Look up the movies in the Sunday *Times*
soon to come or now playing in your neighborhood
theaters.

Read a book about the internal combustion engine
& its relationship to the heart,
ground fog, & antiquated gold stars.

Play chess with my brother, let him
have the queen early in some folly,
my pawns brooding for the rest of the night.

Check all the compound words in the dictionary
thinking of them
lying on the couch which turns into our bed
in your apartment. This is before the bulldozers
come, & the weather light
on the MONY building is steady yellow.
You know what that means.

Pat the cheeks of my three-year-old niece,
let her know I love her
& will go anywhere she wishes, if
she will stop jumping
up & down on my pulse,
& lying to me
about her needs.

Write a contract offering your mother
for the squaw in you,
10 horses, three hands high, each.

All of them smile, & are never
very hungry, & they have teeth like icebergs
at sunset.

Right now I'm mixing a drink
that would have killed Socrates,
& I guess I'll give you a call in a few minutes,
just to see what you're doing.

Fiddling With The Fish
Of Darkness

It was cold.
It was cold & the nights
were crowded with separate bedrooms.
Slight motor sounds,
the fishing boats tug
at their end of the darkness;
fiddling with the fish of darkness.

She took it upon herself to go somewhere
& save us from the tentacles
of adolescence which flap
without bodies all over Spain.
I took it upon myself
to aim for the tree, right over
there, with the car. It is not
being alone which makes your aim accurate;
it is watching your lover placing blankets
over your head when she thinks you are sleeping,
you open your eyes & she explains, "Didn't
want you to get cold." The car never made
the tree, it flipped several times,
& stuttered until
some Spanish teenagers saved me. Remember,
it is three a.m., a lonely road, a
night when you can't even remember where
you parked the car & I am bleeding

& things don't work
the way they were planned to. Two
nurses, the best-looking women in Spain,
hold my penis & I'm peeing. We all
smile at that. The hospital is the same
as all Spain, vacant. A vacant lot,
a vacant john on an airplane, that says,
Vacant. The doctor likes

to lift my arm, dislocated,
& watch me faint. He speaks to me
as if I'm dead & it is not a failure.
The nurses are glad I'm alive,
we will make more water now
just to prove it. They handle things
perfectly. Even my cold balls,
bait for the fish of darkness.
Hungry now for anything.

Spending Your Life
Killing Yourself

It all starts quite early. Maybe
just after you get up, something like
a fluorescent rat dances in your skull,
you have never felt this way about
anything before. Is this good? Is
this bad? You wrap your head in gauze
to keep the swelling down, & also, you know
when injured the first thing is always
the bandaid, & the temperature, 12 in the shade.
Perhaps, tho, you missed your mouth, &
the thermometer dangles from a very large pore
in your face right next to where your mouth
might also be, well, it's not an emergency
& nobody cares anyway.

An airplane glowing like fried mucus
flops into the rat's ear, & you feel
your life is full of small electric
heaters, & perhaps someone has left them on
all night, & if you could put your feet
inside your head, you could warm them up
a little, & winter would not always be
a frozen piece of bread slapped against
the sidewalk

& everyone you know is crying & maybe
this is the reason the plane always has
a hard time of it, nothing, not even
this story is ripped to shreds & everyone
is crying. It just doesn't make sense.
Two artificial lungs, some left-over Spam,
& whatever else you want.

Open Heart Surgery

Suppose you knew someone
who was there

in the middle of open heart surgery,
hanging around, glaring at you,

the doctor turns away for
a moment to sign autographs, this

person drops several green marbles
into your exposed arteries, they feel

like marbles, but you are dizzy, &
not wanting to sound like a fool, or

foul up the doctor's good time,
he keeps saying as you mumble,

"Don't try to talk now," he smiles influentially
into the T.V. camera.

You do not see this person or the doctor
ever again, & as you walk out of the hospital,

it is night, you wanted to do it quietly,
a million fireflies crash into your face,

or maybe they are taking your picture, you've
been saved, both of your hands

flop to the ground like large hot begonias,
a marble rests in the curled waxed petals,

twitching in the cold wet grass, your
arms turn into flamingoes, & you sigh,

"Now, perhaps they will let me die."

Trails

A big handful of snow
in his head. Several animals
are walking. He tracks them
easily. They leave frozen trails.
He skates along them. He pushes
trees aside. Glides into
an opening. They are fast.
They are gone. He is going, too.
Into a deeper clearing. The ground
is mud. So are his eyes. His eyes
are rainbows in the sun.
Several animals dash
under the rainbow. They head
for the cold river,
& tracks as yet undiscovered.

Learning To Love
In America

Dogs & other pets in the country
did the job. Flash, Bingo, & a few nameless
lickers. As a habit, they died chasing cars
or through dread diseases simply dreamed
their lives away.

One ran deer & was shot by hunters
who knew better how dogs
were to live. At ten, I learned of him
at the general store,
"You better watch that goddam dog of yours,
he's gonna get his head blown off one of these days."
I knew very little of men, of deer, & nothing at all
of guns. I did know his half-Beagle carcass
would turn up, rotting, in the woods. Pal.

Always the knots, always the nights, &
"Don't die, mother, I couldn't take it
if you died, mother." A cat would push
under the covers to be put out. Its rough
tongue adding red flesh to my fears. & it would go.

My sister saved the sandbank for small graves.
I would have nothing to do with it.
Markers of wood, & dead animal spirits
put me off. I would hide
high in some warm pine.

My wife's tears come.
Snakes slither through my heart.
The call of a cat is on my ears.
Her teeth are at my wrist. The singing
of ten dogs on a wet night.
I am sick & strange
in a small attic room
& ask to be put to sleep.

Bad Music Continues

Sometimes they tell you everything. Everything.
Santo & Johnny fret & are fretted by
the Hawaiian guitar
the notes continue
long after to waver
& compliment the wine vapors
& how no one named Santo &/
or Johnny
could be forgotten
or remembered
accurately, an operation
of the imagination similar
to the removal of the cyst
from your lip
that has left a scar
which you tell people
has something to do
with your days in the street
listening to bad music
though of course
to get to the streets
you had to hitch rides in old Studebakers
& go ten miles through the woods,
& by the time you got there
everybody had finished fighting
for the day, & was busy
in the drugstore
lifting interesting things & goosing
the girl who had pimples & loved
to be goosed &
stolen from, most of her friends
had rotten teeth, most of their older
brothers & sisters had none at all,
it is easy
to look mean
without teeth. There was a girl
someone fucked

who made you wear two rubbers,
she had little resistance,
people without teeth know about rubbers,
everything there is to know.
They have heard of Santo & Johnny &
probably have a scratched 45
with both of their hits, though
they will never have the money
to see them in person,
& have more important things to do:
staring in the mirror,
& fingers run down the wedged scars,
as authentic as any world.

Winter Light

Old snow litters the streets,
& some fire snorts in the dump.
It has been a quiet time. Finding
things to use for the winter. Finding

things that can be disposed of easily,
without harm to the present body
which seems also to be made of disposable fabric
the texture of waffles
caught in teeth & tasteless.

It is too early to say some of the arteries
have gone
where dead arteries go, tho
the lungs under x-ray
etch out streets of darkness
with names you won't recall.

Animal Dream

I am fifty-five
on my way to retirement.
I have bought a swamp in Florida.
I am a flamingo
on someone else's lawn. I am
a swan in someone else's
dark garden. I am the mainstay
in the brilliant used car lot. I am
the dregs, the beer vat, the end of the year.
I am a feather plucker out to lunch.
I am straightening out the wind
with my teeth. I rise into fire,
& come back rare. Stars rust
in the water of my eyes, I have run
to the end of my world.

Streets

A car is opened
up
like a squirrel
on the street.

Aren't you ever coming home?
I could bleed all night
like an auto wreck
or an unsure animal
who
missed
the obvious limb which
wavers
in the black sky.

The Satanic American Flag

Or Goofing In My Dune Buggy Drinking Beer,
Throwing Moons, & Generally Offending Everybody

1 So's I don't die, fall down dead
in my tracks, 9AAA,

I run at em & stuff
my flag into their nostrils

& as you all know
that'll kill, or stop

just about any enemy
wearing shin guards or not

that I know. Oh I know
some people like to fuck around

with/on our flag & I've heard
that that flag, I can't reveal

the source, is a contraceptive
device if used properly

it brings on a premature menopause
which pleases all those people

who are serious about controlling
population & such

which is why it's also a good reason to
wipe out some more of those gooks & whatchamacallits,

If we could get this country back
to around thirteen states

we wouldn't have to sweat
land, wars, laws,

& the small children who come
offering warm bombs in soft flags.

2 The thick taste of the flag
  is not mother's milk.

3 A flag rises like a piece of bad magic.
  You follow the trick.
  You know what happens next.
  A small breeze & everyone stirs
  like they have found a witch
  & it is a dull day in Salem.

4 You happen to be lying
  in the center of the grand old flag

  & you ask several people
  to enclose you,

  fold you up in it, tie
  some white ribbon around the top

  & you are quite legal,
  certainly not wearing a flag,

  you are captured by it, but
  still, you say in a muffled

  voice, trying to prove something,
  "Take me to Niagara Falls,

  this hunk a cloth is stronger,
  more tough than five barrels."

  There is a short fire fight
  in your head as you hum

  the soggy version of your favorite
  flag song.

5 He gets horny often if he is a flag
  he wants to fuck everything he can get
  his hands on.

6 How to design a national flag:
Color—unimportant, make it a little jazzy
if you want it to stand out in the movies,
Fabric—unimportant, if you feel the country has some
kind of future you might want to make it of durable
material, if not, cardboard flags are as good as
anything,
Length & Width—The most important aspect of designing
your flag. Now what you do, you take the average height
of the males of your country, add two inches for every
hundred years you figure your country'll last, allow
plenty of room for getting fat, & that's it, you've got
yourself the perfect casket cover.

7 Things not to get hot about:
In my red wet-look camouflage outfit

topped off with a basic blue
"Visit Mt. Shasta and/or

Angkor Vat" cap,
& a doily white chest

filled with a heart of gold.

8 One day you are quite alone
& hungry, perhaps in a swamp of your own making,

Hungry, so you take your flag out,
put it between two hunks of Tip Top bread,

break open a bottle of Italian Swiss Colony
wine, & there you are,

feeding yourself,
a long way from home

eating the flag is not
like eating your heart out. What you fear

is things won't settle right
& you'll be action-painting

the soil of some foreign land
with your hideous colors

& you know, christ,
they'll never understand.

9 After many months of this kind of dreaming
his eyes turned to flags.

Sometimes, he would have to flip
his head up so they wouldn't

drag on the ground. On
occasion, fires would suddenly

erupt, for no reason &
something would burn higher

& hotter than the dump. He found
beauty is sometimes not

in the eye of the beholder.

10 There is a white flag
dangling from your back pocket.

Use it.

Gold, The Peace Of Space

Light broke in your body.
Why does the figure fly toward the sun;
why does the figure fly toward the sea?

The gold eyes take a long walk into the night,
they fire small volleys
at the stars, things tumble
forever. Ducks in a
shooting gallery.

I rise with you,
learning the peace
of space. The gun
sleeps like an old stove;
the stove sleeps, a river of
gold birds in your belly;
your belly of gold stars.

I am going there,
going there, armed, knowing
no other way.

Trying To Be Relevant
In America

I am a grease ball. I finger shirt collars.
I am so greasy, I slide
down windows & only
slip back in time
to fill teenage faces
with blackheads,
the night of the big dance.
I am the wax that dribbles from your ears.
I am the crud between your teeth
after a big slab of ham.
I am the priest of your nostrils
as your sinuses flow
with the weather.
I am the miracle of your hair
three days asleep
on your head.
I am the grease of your heart
swelling
as you touch the fat thigh
of your own true love.

The Innkeeper's Daughter

The innkeeper's daughter
wears herself thin
in the service
of the earth. Apple orchards
pass through her eyes
like fire trucks
warming up on Sundays
in a dry country.

It was an era of final trains
& speeches made of sour wood.

She slips off into the cold foliage
of blue fire. To sit down

to pump up the soil,
to swallow the long tunes
of stone.

Nearly Blonde

Your blonde, nearly blonde,
hair tangles in my mouth,
I do not worry about strangulation.

I hold the eyes of the soundless yellow
night animals
in my arms.

The nightmare sighs, I have come home,
I have come home.

Occupying Space

Occupying the space
you left one hundred years ago
& returning with a toothbrush
in one pocket, a spray deodorant
under the arm, & the feces of
twenty quite ordinary women.

The power you enacted was orange
sun in black windows, orange sun
sick in deep green eyes, the power
was a taxi vomiting itself
into the river, & flies fought
for a taste.

You were not without love or
sodium, tho no one thought
you would ever leave the city
& find a seat on the train. No
message, no trees, or hiking boots,
no spine that will not freeze. No one
spoke of lockjaw, tho some said skin
shrivels, & there is not a great
appetite when you are taking up
room.

Everything was a waste of time;
socks covering up stumps, medication
for the glowing bowels, stamps for
letters that would get lost. Slipping
into a cluttered haze, you parted
with yourself for awhile, having said
goodby, thirty or forty times. A splinter
was in your spine, it would shatter
or rise.

The Gypsy & His Best Friends

The women braid reeds together. It may be
a large boat or a small house
when they get finished. It may be both.
One of the ladies on the left, says,
to the lady on the furthest right, "Is that
a rudder?" "No, it's a fireplace, you
fool." & days go on this way, almost
as if the brains were drooling the last
sample of order. A gypsy comes along in his cart,
& drags off the youngest of the women, perhaps,
95, her reeds drift behind the cart
like so much bad rubbish, she has been here before,
she thinks. With her last few remaining reeds
she weaves something very similar to the
contemporary cocoon, & that is where they
set up their household. The gypsy, Rex, would say,
"to hell with modern conveniences, I've got you,
Amanda, & my boa constrictor, Felix." Felix was an
eyesore, or that's the way Amanda conceived of him.
When guests came to the cocoon, you had to hang
him up on his hook. His hook was in the shape
of a large baby, & he would flex his muscles, & really,
he loved his hook. But Amanda being a high & mighty
weaver of reed houses &/or boats & something
of a socio-psychopath, thought Felix was an eyesore.

The Short Sad Story
Of The Skin Graft

A nylon dress, a sheath, blue,
shimmers,

the soft walls, a deep red,
cocktails, strong, served by

the waiter in residence, warmed
the eyes, & she danced, everyone

knew under it all, the charm, the
flamboyance, she was partly naked,

tho they were not sure her breasts had
nipples, or her upper thighs smiled, or

curling hair, & there was they knew
definitely an odor of wormy earth

whenever she moved. In one graceless
twirl she bruised the candle, fabric

& stomach flesh merged. Pores still flow
tho you will never hear from her again,

someone is working around the clock
as usual, new patterns are engaging,

sometimes glowing, mending raw meat,
& eyes never reward the weavers, or

gather slipped stitches. Small mountains
rise like geodesic domes in the hot

but quiet valley of death.

The Thick Knife

He loved her in simple ways, with simple fingers,
& yet we spoke of children
with hair like sand,

He threw slabs of fat, self-contempt
& yet we spoke of children's eyes
dust-filled in the darkness,

The edge of the knife is thick.
The rooms are narrow & blue.

He was frightened
of scar tissue
& kept picking them up
in the simplest acts . . .

The children grow faint
as he chases the wallpaper, kisses the
oily floor, lights up a
long cigarette

& braids her fine blonde hair
tightly, blood sweats through,
& animals, small, & unhealthy,
quiver.

Pouring Yourself

Pouring yourself out of a glass
into someone's mouth

I re-enter your life. There is
a bird, so quiet he has

died & is about
to live as something else.

When I wake into the ashes
of your hair, inhaling deeply,

I know better
where things lead

when you have emptied yourself,
the coif tumbles like soiled clothes

or a gold braid dangling from
a seventh story window, frozen

& silent as a chair
on a flagpole. Oh, it is still there,

come, sit awhile, relax your tired arms,
let wind pass through you. I find

myself posed with an opera singer
about to expose her lungs, she

has poise, I have poise, when
we die we will no longer need

to gargle dust, & weeds hum
open all our raw tunnels.

Pounding On The Doors

A short novel made in America

1 American Novel: Self-Taught

It loves to be touched a lot.
It will touch you
it appears. It craves a slap
on the wrist. Sometimes
it will let you hug it gently
without lust or understanding.
It is surely a repetitious virgin
growling at the vortex.
It is hanging in a tree right now,
Only its symbols are left.
It is deep winter
in the heart of the novel.
It is symmetrical & you've been there before
on a hot day in July with the top down
& the radio crying for its lovers.

2 The Real Muzzy

Everybody is swimming. You didn't
reckon on this. To immerse yourself
in these waters is to carry a fat burden
you didn't know existed
until just a few minutes ago.
The swimming pool is warm &
the casual freedom tastes of blood,
& you've just about had your fill.
It is raining locust, they are
in the act of breeding. You will
call them a delicacy & weave them into
your next tapestry, & serve them
on Sunday as a hunk of edible art.
Everyone will delight & feel the whole thing
has been worth it. The struggle, the climb,
the vats of grease you must lug to the

mountains in the Ponce de Leon forest. Do you
remember the peacocks there, sprouting
like birthmarks on the young skin of trees?
They were serene phantoms. What a feast, it was,
you were an angel smoking twigs, & you said,
Oh WoW, with one eye, opening & closing
like a picture window suddenly
taking pictures. Your eyelashes
were the fans of life
making things comfortable & I thought
I would die in solitude, up a tree
& wingless in the dawn of friendly persuasion.
We saw beavers building dams from rushes
along the river, it was high time
we came down to earth. I tied their tails together &
made you
lie on the coat. We sailed through dusty vineyards
crushing grapes with our bellies.
Our bellies had been small & hungry.
You seemed depressed. There had to be
at least hope or water
over that foaming hill. A canoe perhaps
in the morning calling for us
at the front door.
The lilacs give our house that picture postcard look.
We feel enchanted, tiny, hidden away,
as we are in our little love nest
with the beavers & swans
& the quonset hut mist
always apparent.

3 The Knotty Revelation

He has seen everything. He has been with everything
at one time or another.

A fire in his lungs turns
to women dancing. He pokes them
with his trigger finger. They giggle
& continue unfolding yard after yard
of slinky fabric. It is good soft material
though it produces an intense heat,
& he knows he has been warm.
He knows a barter when he sees one
coming. He offers wheat, wheat of his eyes.
They take it in their teeth like spaghetti.
They smile, it is better than spaghetti.
They see a good deal is at hand. They massage
his sore legs for hours & the wheat
sways full,
& ready for the cropping. Soon the house
will burst with wonderful toothpicks.
Small red stones
drool in his head.

4 Pounding On The Doors

A pounding on every door.
Someone wanted information.
No one knew, nobody
kept anything in the closet.
No one had thought of safe-cracking tools
in a while, & they
were probably in the closet.
All other violations. Everyone slipped
some change under the doors.
A humming of marbles, a humming of exits,
a humming of fists, a humming of metal.
Is there no end in sight,
they sigh.

5 Afterword

We thought about weddings. Smoked dope
& fought off complicated relationships
with the fireplace. Matchbook covers
led us to the edge of new occupations.
We knew the misery of money, got caught
up in the liberation of our language.
We went into analysis, quit writing,
opened up bookstores to be near the
words. We sold subscriptions to the
Grail Quest, passed out of ourselves
gulping mead in a backwoods cafe, "Help
Me Make It Through The Night," wailed
& reduced us to garbled tears. We
found ourselves touched
by young men piled on a raft heading
downstream toward the moonlight. A silent
but very beautiful woman drags
her fingers of white bone
through the muck & the murk. Not even
a note of hope in bad scrawl. Her dandruff
is as close as we come to rice paper. She
is a rich & happy widow. When she combs
her soggy hair, peat moss smoulders, &
the tree of lost things spreads
that wildfire.

The Rump Roast
& What Happened

The rump roast was in the oven. I was thinking.
The angel in the apple tree, how she
looked like god, she blended so easily
with the scenery, & this was something different.
There we were in the corn belt &
someone was burning their draft card,
& of course, going to jail, though
they didn't know then
what jail was; the life of jail.

Setting myself aflame,
at least my shirt in a padded cell, having flooded
the first, I sang
Brahmin hymns I made up as I went along
with jail. At this point,
they called the psychiatrist.
We sat & chatted in a small room,
until I noticed the two-way mirror.
I wrote in spit, Fuck You,
as loud as I could, a thousand birds
fluttered from the words
& got lost in the night.
So drunk, so disorderly, & so secure,
"We've never seen anybody as crazy as him,"
they told everybody but me.

Kelly came, a little confused,
good friends always are. We had a laugh
for an hour. How I had attacked
the cow's apartment, not her, but the herness
of her: the T.V. (with a chair), the telephone
(with a broom), the record player (with my foot),
the sewing machine (with my hands).
Plastic flew everywhere like angels.
So did her boyfriend, I believe,
a rookie monk. Her roommate,

an inveterate cowgirl sang a weird ballad
I hope I never hear again. I saw guitars
in her eyes, as they slapped the cuffs
around my wrists, they were twanging, too.
The cow thought they had come to change
her hay. She cried
at the loss. & waited
for the eternal milking.

Syl thought I needed a good shake,
but we had breakfast instead.
I was happy not to be at home,
though I knew the oven was still on,
& by now the fumes
had caused delicious visions
to rise
throughout that whole world.

Aroused Prurient Interests

She demands to be unhappy.
She'd even straighten the ears of the rabbit.
Pulling until his brains fell like balls.
She demands to be unhappy.
In her ears, smut smut, all is smut.
The conspiracy, the conspiracy
is bruising her children
like pears. She trots
to the President of the University,
"A boy in my class, writing, writes
some of the dirtiest words
you could imagine."

& her husband, coaxed,
fucks the daylight out of her
in some weird barn
on a warm romantic fall afternoon.

She fires all of her teachers,
dances, tortures her children.
In the world, all the cocks soar
to fill her pursed lips.

Rules

Let the roads
quietly die.

Let the birds
cracking through the firs
find room for their wings.

More Rules

Take the sloppy coins from his eyes
Put a ring of fire in his nose

Tell it to the blue spruce
Go back into your own bland history

Fill her up
Promulgate mysteries

Do not drive while drunk
Eke out a living

A lit cigarette in the cellar
A foray into the eyes of the woods

You will remember this as long as you live
As long as you live

Travis, The Kid Was All Heart

You watched out for him or
you got your mouth messed up.

Orthodontist was not a word he
hauled around behind his mauler's
eyes. He liked to fuck sheep &

eat spiders. When he slept, he
farted toads. In those games of touch

football, his feet would send your balls
back where they belonged. A friendly
slap on the ass was "fag stuff." He'd

goose you forever with everything he had,
Coke bottles, brooms, or his rough nose.

In the huddle he'd call for plays involving
several pubescent girls, electric toothbrushes,
multiple vitamins, & honey. We'd lap

it all up. The rubbers in our wallets
wobbled like failed field goal attempts.

Downfield, he always caught the pass on his
fingertips. Defensive ends, guards, & backs
humped the earth for him.

Some teeth raked the fur of his calves, some
teeth crunched having found themselves

trapped in his simple sidestep. He cut
roses all the way to the wounded moon
lying on her back waiting, fuck yes, waiting.

The Woman
Of The Wilderness

The woman of the wilderness wears
white stockings & several shares of AT&T.
She has propensity
for camouflage similar to that
of the army private, branches sprout
from her hair, mud glows in her large pores,
& none of her weapons are concealed.

At the marketplace, the woman of the wilderness
haggles, haggles
& as the sun decides to double her form
she waddles away,
weaves through the trees
hunting for a good night's rest,
baby teeth clinking,
clinking near her neck.

Dreary Tides,
The Vast Hot House
Of The Mind

Just a short note: Literature &
cold coffee. Dreams piped in, & you
don't have to form questions. T.V. &
slick magazines have been explained.
She allows no human contact as it
probably wouldn't be good. The
current is free, the synapses are
frozen. A dog in the snow, blood
at its nose, a slow-motion nosebleed,
a brilliant stream of death that
goes on forever encased in a thin
icicle. I've gotten carried away, it's
the weather. The mailbox is frozen
for the duration. & the goldfish died,
how can you talk about a goldfish, white,
lying on its side, & light splintering
its skin, & the one spot where its
breathing sac is/was, red, & the breaks
in your life, frozen goldfish snapped in
half by small fingers, not meaning to
break anything but just bad fingers & sentimental
as heather jolted out of context, heather
gone mad in the sun eating cantaloupe,
sucking cherries, some heather just
sitting around forever gnawing on
warm gooseberry tendons.

Exhausted After Years

Your thin blonde hair smokes in the ashtray.
Strategically, I move
this room into another room
without paintings of small children
lapping up the walls. Orange candles
melt on white porcelain, green leaves
clutch the inevitable spaces
that come when you turn away. I
have purchased a solid wristwatch, I
learn the days in the morning with eggs.
I am capable of pulling myself
inside out, for one reason
or another. I scrub the filth
of my lungs with sandpaper, my fingers
are heated tunnels I use to
crumble up eyes
which lodge under the feet
like quartz exhausted after years
of preparation & dry-runs & damaged
material sold cheaply after
the sprinkler system
discharged, spraying a thin rain
of blood on the blue velour. We brought it
home, not complaining, & wrapped ourselves,
two cold presents for an antiquated
mother who lies down
like rough wood with us
for the rest of our natural lives.

A Man All Grown Up
Is Supposed To

The anger rises with metal filings &
I will not see the ground as rock &
the stones will not carry my rubber spirit.
I have hit nothing in months & the candle
stuffed in my stomach flaps fire, flaps
smoke, goes out. I have no money, I am
very sorry about that, it would make things
easier, I suppose. A man all grown up is
supposed to have a pocket full wherever he
is, & feed his woman & kiss the teeth of
the fire & dance with the trucks & pitch
pennies with the soft children.

When his anger collected he found the dog's
rubber bone, he chewed on it in the corner,
growling at the cat, the children, the night
of impetigo. She took it away, saying, come
inside. It's cold out there, come inside
before you catch your death of cold, he knew
what she meant, he knew & tore the hair off
her head, the moon was harmless & so pale.

He sighed with the moths, & asked the
linoleum, for god's sake, forgive, his
fingers rolled around in the sink under
the hard water, & her eyes were a deer
carcass out in the woods, no one around,
no one ever there when you need them.

Tapping

You crack open trees
searching for squirrels, something

to touch with love. I go
into that night without

reservations & grab the words
of a woman who suffers, softly,

from venereal warts, her boyfriend
is down the coast pulling fish

from the Mediterranean & the
Spanish undercover agent peers

over his purple sunglasses, hoping
for a whore hustling, or some dope

changing hands. Our conversation
extends to the burning rain, the

raucous loud speakers & I tap
out all the silences of my life.

The Philadelphia Story

You are short, soft,
& in Philadelphia, talking to
your favorite cousin. Soon, you will
reach the point of sleep. You will think
how mad I was last night, the demonic
son of a bitch, telling you
you knew nothing. You remind me
of the orange way I have with everything.
I burn a little at that.

Tonight, you are eating Philadelphia cream cheese,
& I am glowing still. I want to tell you,
a fellow wrote to me today about my poems,
saying, I was too angry
to make art, that three years ago,
Sunday, his home-made house
in Colorado burned, & he's been
smoking ever since.

You let your hands
calm my fever, tho, tonight
all the brotherly love in the world
is not enough. Did you sleep on
the train? Did the train sleep in you?
& what of me
will keep you warm
when the fuming clock strikes itself
like angels discovering their arms, their legs,
their simple fires.

Could We Live

Could we live in, could we make it
in a room that looks like a fire hydrant?

Other nights, the Astrodome
on Astro Turf, I want

your buttocks to know grass that
lives forever, green, melting under you;

the scoreboard filled with hot roosters
cracking up every time
I come—this was no home run,

this was floundering in your arms,
wondering where to place myself
for safe-keeping
& as if that was not good enough

I have caught a cold from the sky,
I am pouring out my life again,

You said I looked awful this morning,
what are you going to do about it?

A Note About the Author

Terry Stokes was born in Flushing, New York, in
1943 and grew up in Connecticut. He graduated
from the University of Hartford and has an M.F.A.
degree in Creative Writing from the University of Iowa.
His poems have been published in collections,
broadsides, and various magazines; Cat's Pajamas
Press to *Esquire*. Mr. Stokes is currently Poet-in-
Residence at the University of Hartford.

A Note on the Type

The text of this book has been set by film in a type
face called Claro Light. Actually, Claro is the name
given one of the film versions of Helvetica—perhaps
the most widely accepted and generally acclaimed
sans-serif face of all time. Designed by M. Miedinger
in the 1950's in Switzerland and named for its country
of origin, Helvetica was first introduced in America
in 1963.

The book was composed by University Graphics, Inc.,
Shrewsbury, New Jersey; printed and bound by The
Book Press, Brattleboro, Vermont; designed by Betty
Anderson.